Color the letters Aa and an Alligator

Trace and write an uppercase A:

Trace and write a lowercase a:

Color the letter Bb and a Bear

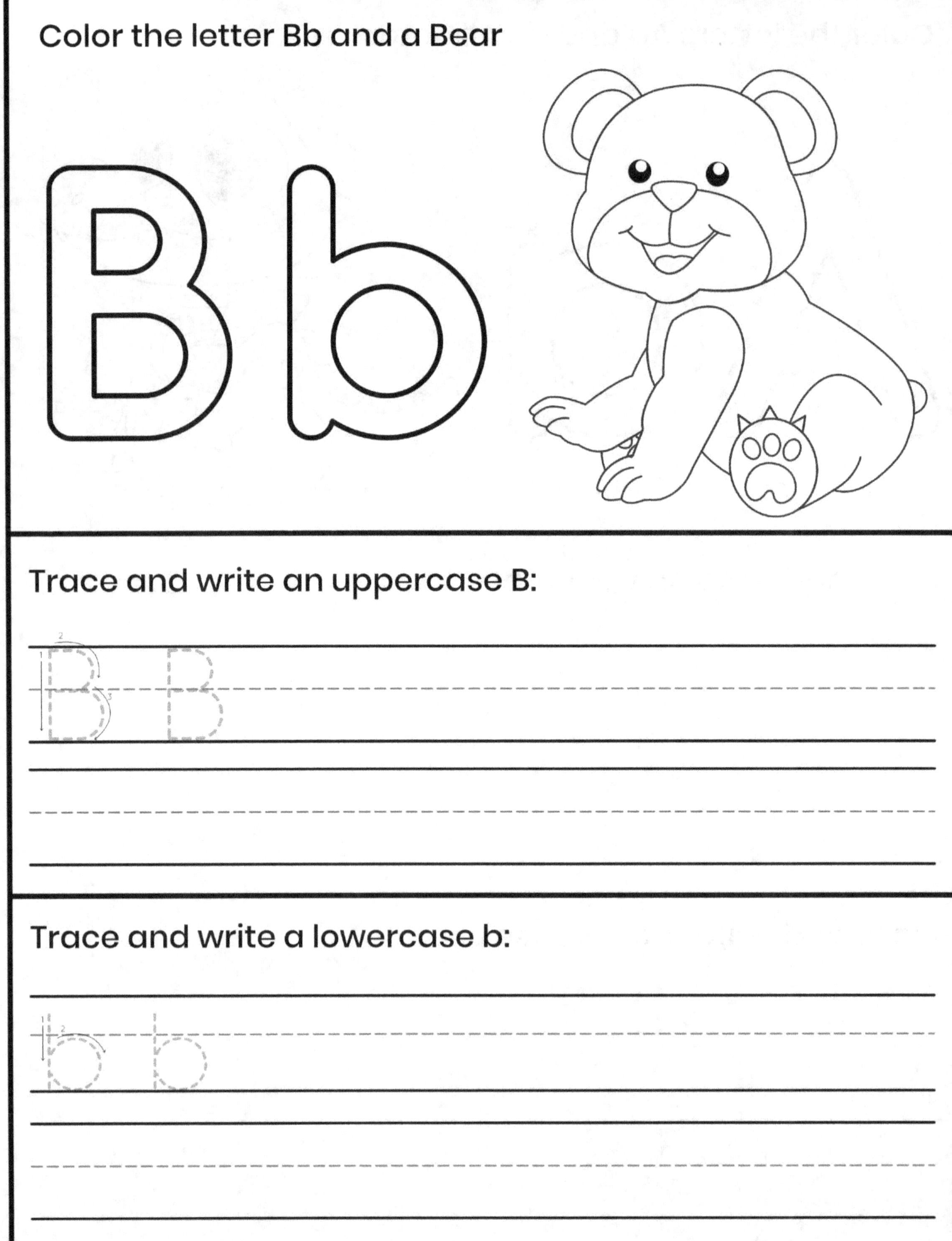

Trace and write an uppercase B:

Trace and write a lowercase b:

Color the letter Cc and a Cat

Trace and write an uppercase C:

Trace and write a lowercase c:

Color the letter Dd and a Dolphin

Trace and write an uppercase D:

Trace and write a lowercase d:

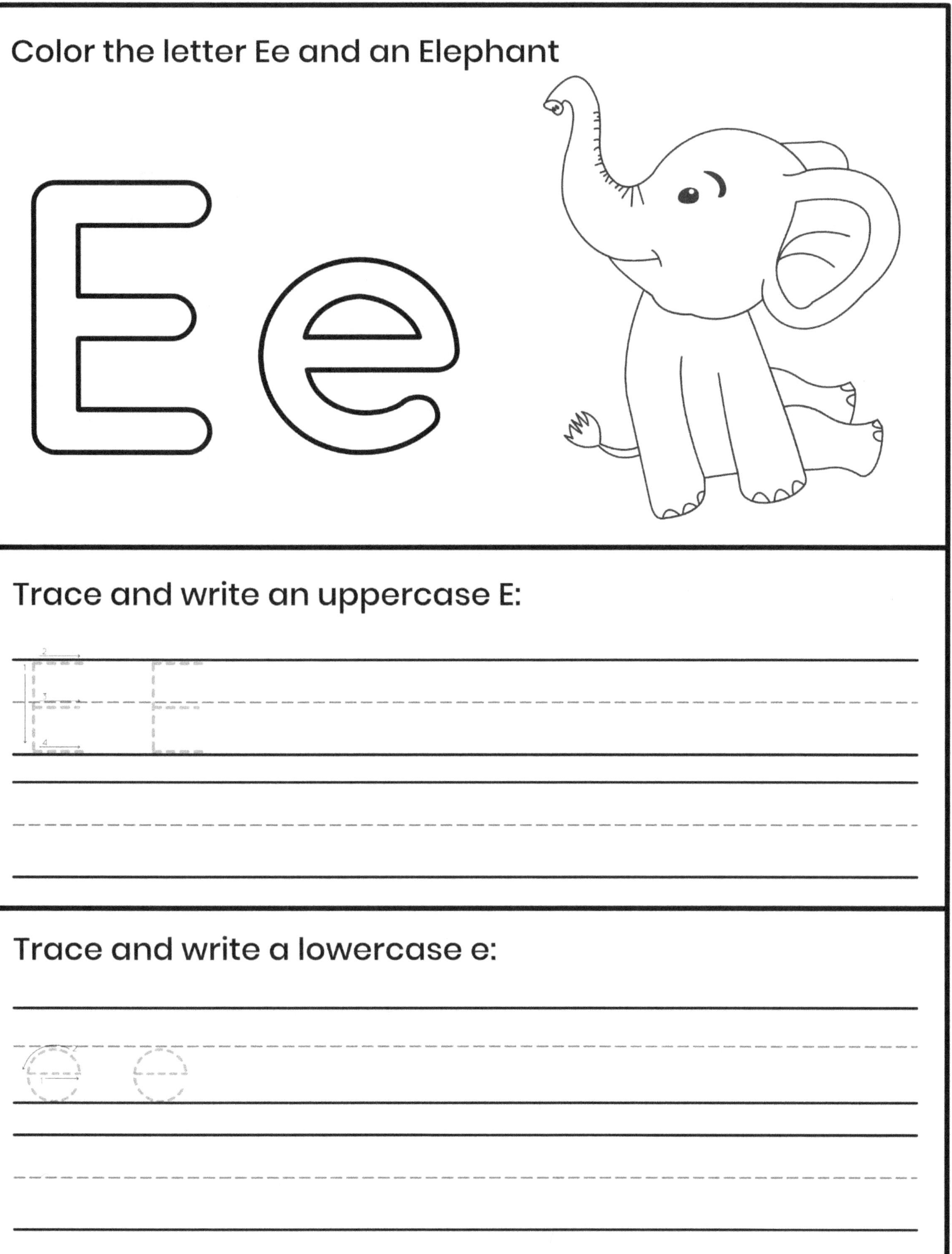

Color the letter Ee and an Elephant

E e

Trace and write an uppercase E:

Trace and write a lowercase e:

Color the letter Ff and a Frog

F f

Trace and write an uppercase F:

Trace and write a lowercase f:

Color the letter Gg and a Giraffe

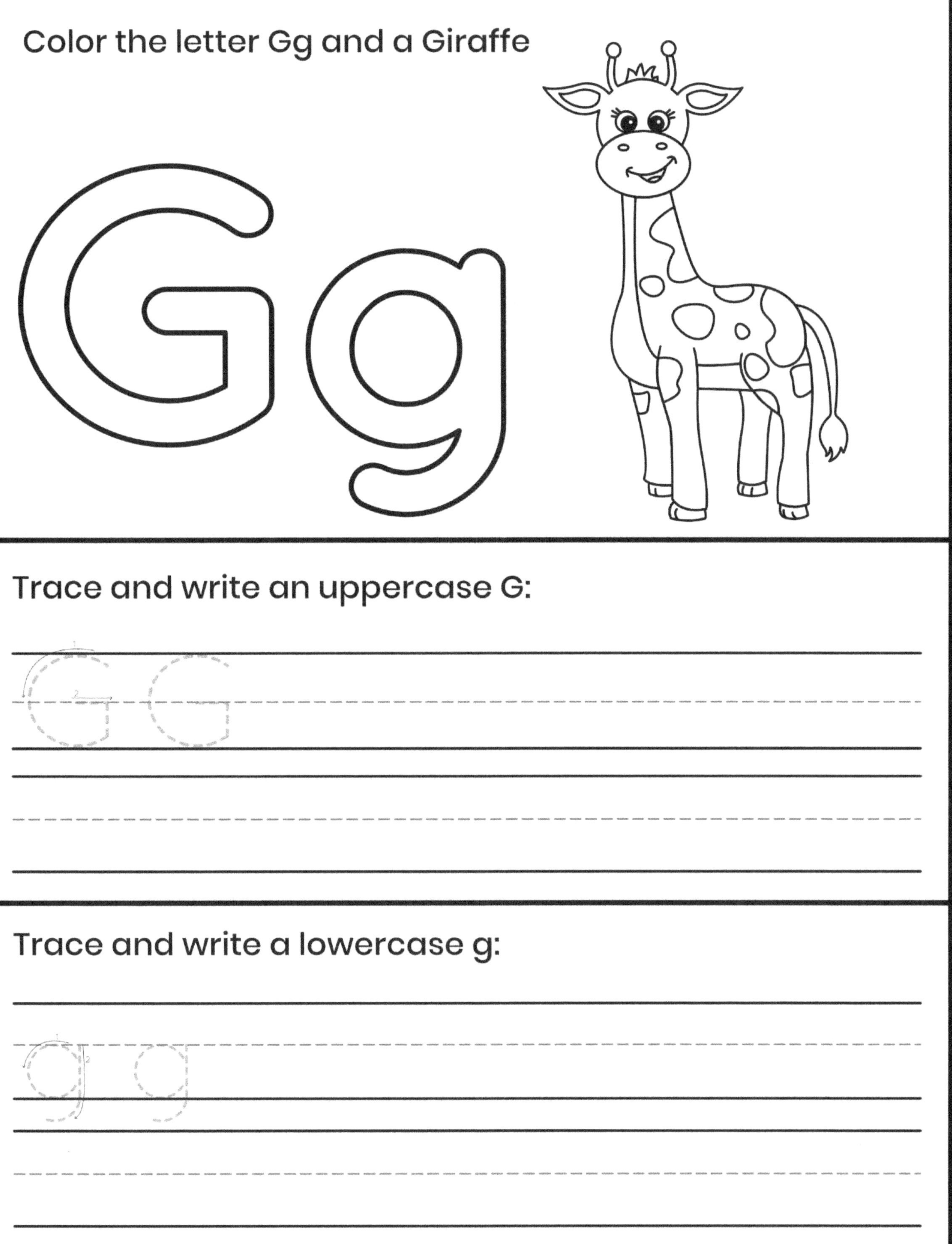

Trace and write an uppercase G:

Trace and write a lowercase g:

Color the letter Hh and a Hippo

Trace and write an uppercase H:

Trace and write a lowercase h:

Color the letter Ii and an Iguana

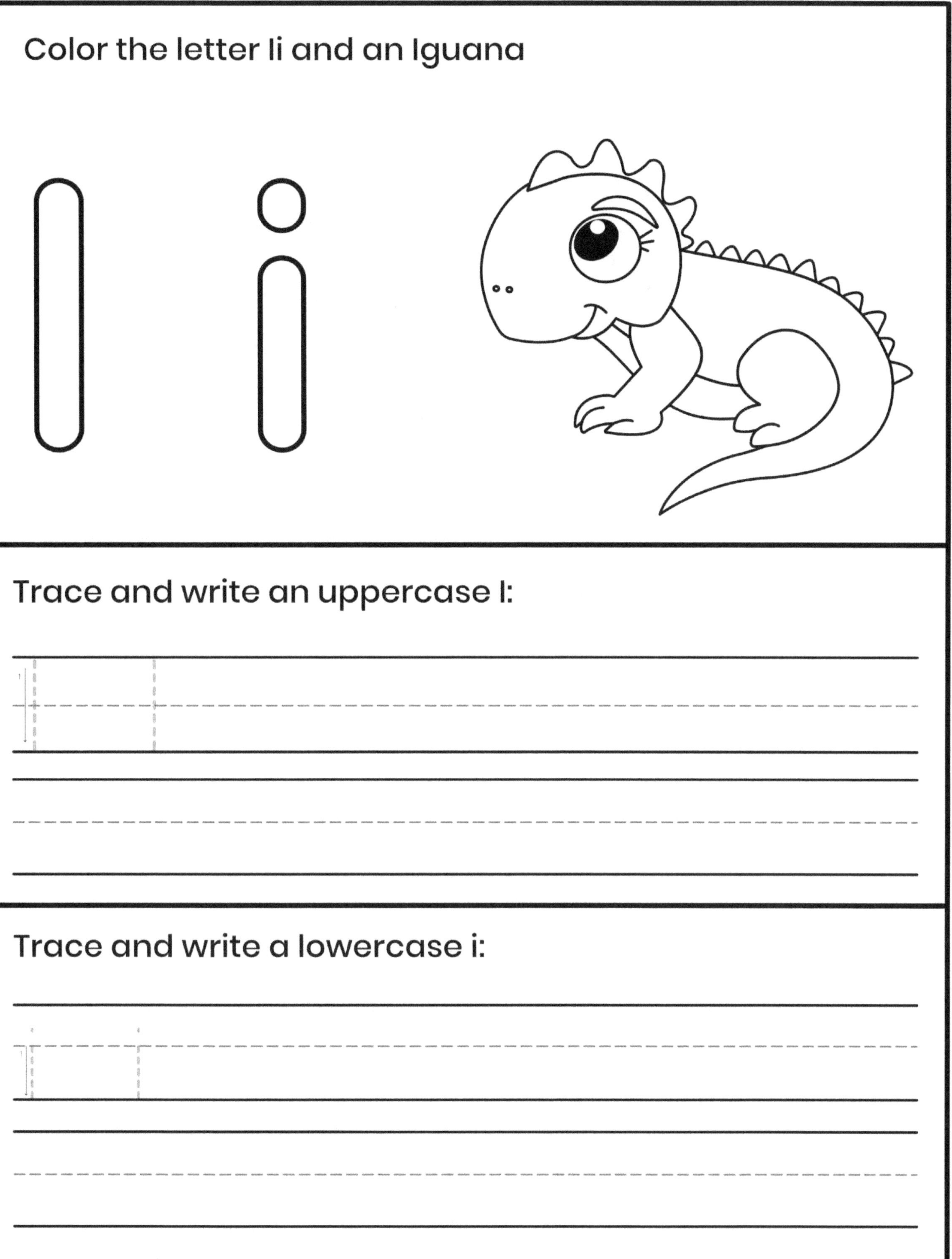

Trace and write an uppercase I:

Trace and write a lowercase i:

Color the letter Jj and a Jaguar

Trace and write an uppercase J:

Trace and write a lowercase j:

Color the letter Kk and a Koala

Trace and write an uppercase K:

Trace and write a lowercase k:

Color the letter Ll and a Lion

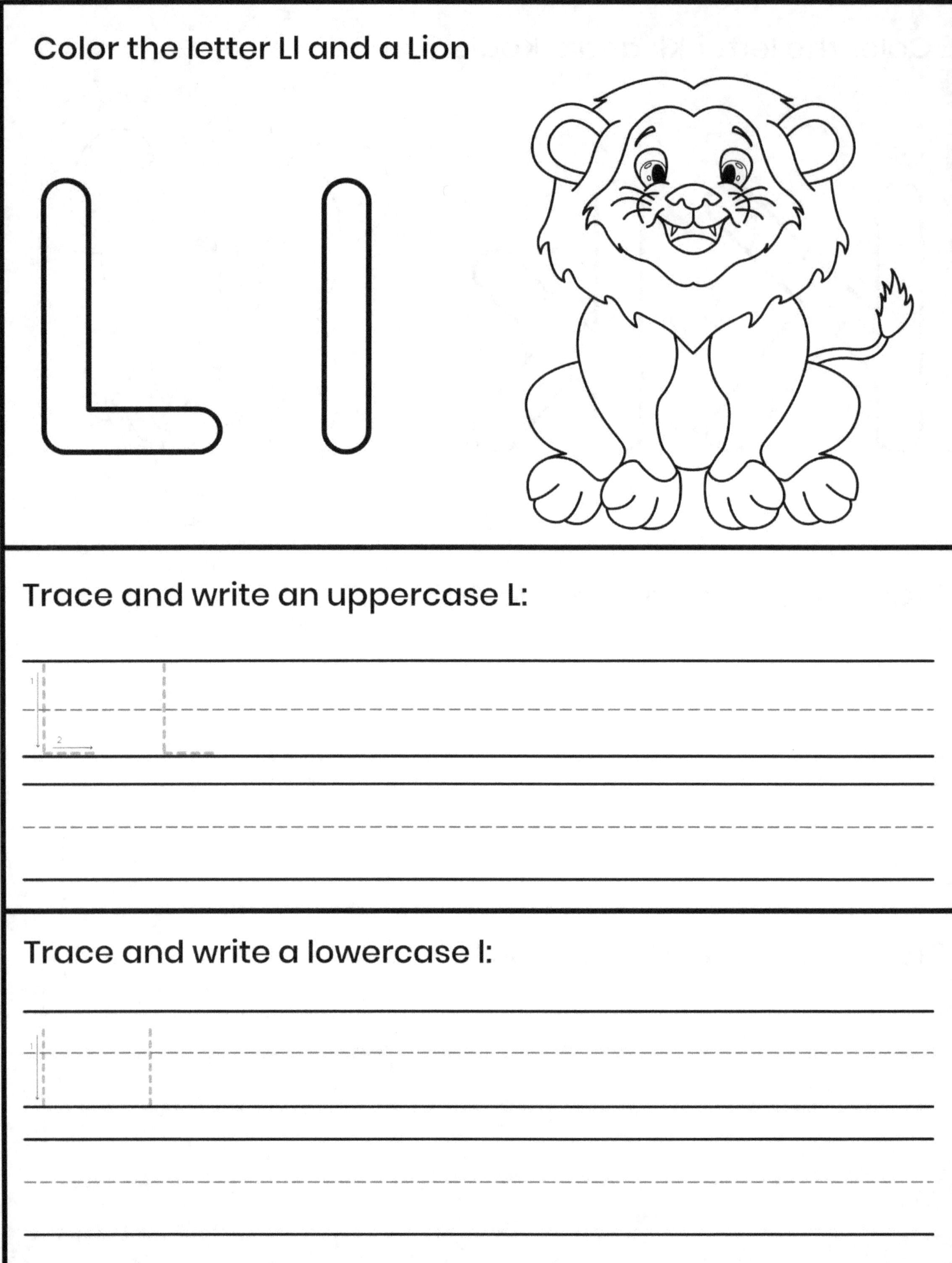

Trace and write an uppercase L:

Trace and write a lowercase l:

Color the letter Mm and a Monkey

Trace and write an uppercase M:

Trace and write a lowercase m:

Color the letter Nn and a Narwhal

Trace and write an uppercase N:

Trace and write a lowercase n:

Color the letter Oo and an Owl

Trace and write an uppercase O:

Trace and write a lowercase o:

Color the letter Pp and a Penguin

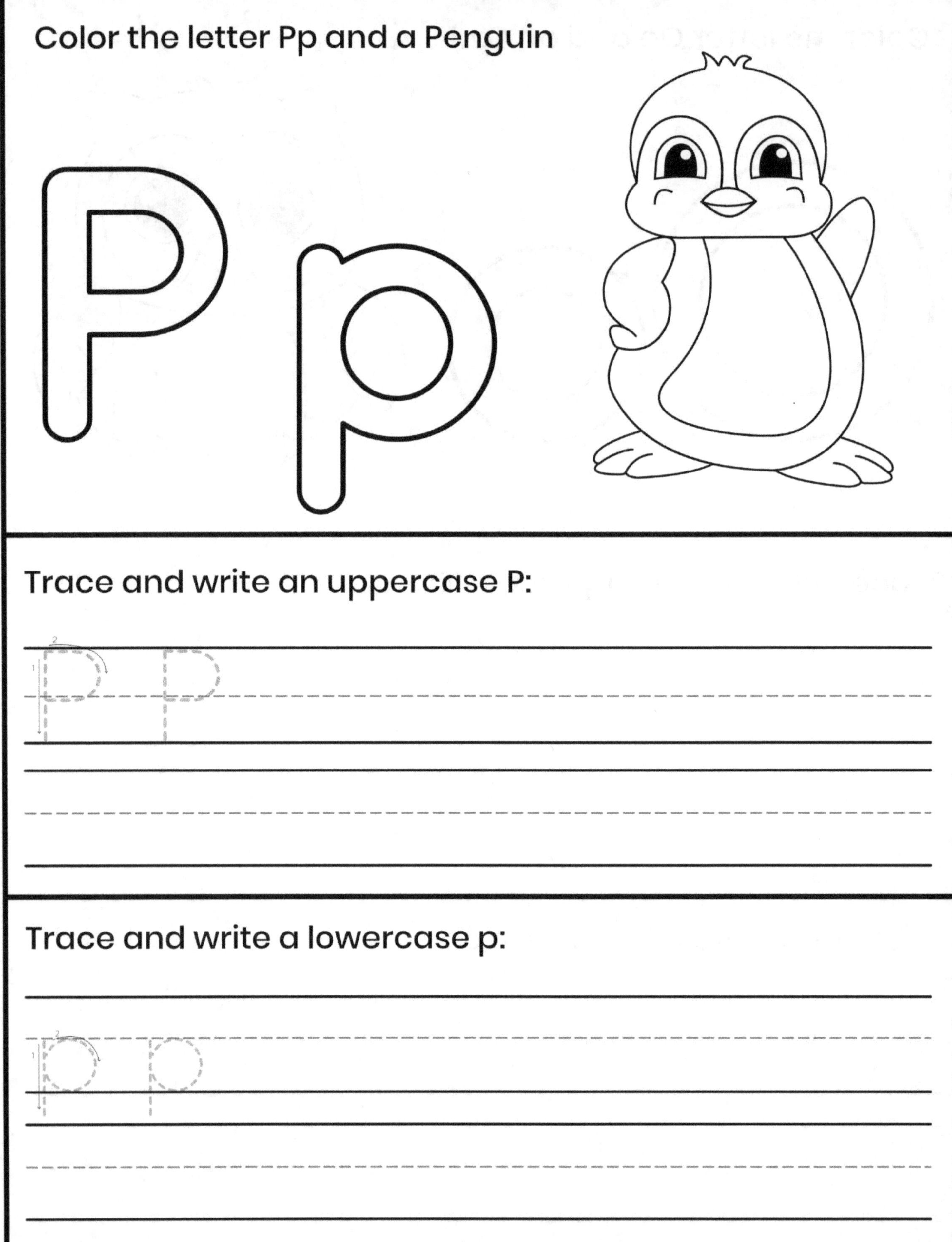

Trace and write an uppercase P:

Trace and write a lowercase p:

Color the letter Qq and a Quokka

Trace and write an uppercase Q:

Trace and write a lowercase q:

Color the letter Rr and a Rabbit

Trace and write an uppercase R:

Trace and write a lowercase r:

Color the letter Ss and a Snake

S s

Trace and write an uppercase S:

Trace and write a lowercase s:

Color the letter Tt and a Tiger

Trace and write an uppercase T:

Trace and write a lowercase t:

Color the letter Uu and an Unicorn

Trace and write an uppercase U:

Trace and write a lowercase u:

Color the letter Vv and a Viper

Trace and write an uppercase V:

Trace and write a lowercase v:

Color the letter Ww and a Whale

Ww

Trace and write an uppercase W:

Trace and write a lowercase w:

Color the letter Xx and a Xerus

X x

Trace and write an uppercase X:

Trace and write a lowercase x:

Color the letter Yy and a Yak

Trace and write an uppercase Y:

Trace and write a lowercase y:

Color the letter Zz and a Zebra

Z z

Trace and write an uppercase Z:

Trace and write a lowercase z: